CHANGE AND GROW

KITTEN TO CAT

Acknowledgements: Cover: getty images/Patricia Doyle, getty images/Marc Henrie, gettyimages/Dorling Kindersley, gettyimages/Vincenzo Lombardo, gettyimages/Marc Henrie. p1 gettyimages/Jane Burton, p2 gettyimages/Dorling Kindersley, p3 gettyimages/Peety Cooper, p4 gettyimages/Jane Burton, p5 gettyimages/3D4Medical.com, pp6–7 gettyimages/Jane Burton, p8 gettyimages/Michael Blann, p9 gettyimages/Steve Gorton and Tim Ridley, gettyimages/Jane Burton, p10 gettyimages/Jane Burton, p11 gettyimages/Steve Shott, p12 gettyimages/ Vincenzo Lombardo, p13 gettyimages/Dorling Kindersley, p14 getty/images/GK Hart/Vikki Hart, p15 gettyimages/Dorling Kindersley, gettyimages/Jane Burton, p16 gettyimages/Koki Iino, gettyimages/TSI Pictures, p17 gettyimages/Jane Burton, p18 gettyimages/Jane Burton, p19 gettyimages/Martin Ruegner, p20 gettyimages/Steve Gorton and Tim Ridley, gettyimages/Ove Eriksson, p21 gettyimages/Sharon Dominick, p22 gettyimages/Stockbyte, p23 gettyimages/Kevin Fitzgerald, p24 gettyimages/Peety Cooper.

First published by Parragon in 2009

Parragon
Queen Street House
4 Queen Street
Bath BA1 1HE, UK

ISBN 978-1-4075-8044-9

Printed in China

CHANGE AND GROW
KITTEN TO CAT

LIVE. LEARN. DISCOVER.

Steve Parker

PaRragon

Bath • New York • Singapore • Hong Kong • Cologne • Delhi • Melbourne

LiFE BEGiNS

**The female cat had her first kittens last summer.
Now it's spring and she is ready to have some more.**

Getting together

At first, the female cat does not like the male cat—in fact she spits at him! But after a while they get together and mate.

The male and female cat may not look alike.

The very beginning
The new kittens begin life as tiny dots, as small as the one on this letter "i."

Safe inside
The kittens grow inside the mother's body, in a baglike part of the body called the womb, or uterus.

Brain

Stomach

Liver Lungs

Intestines

Food pipe and windpipe

Womb

Heart

GROWING INSIDE

The tiny kitten grows fast inside its mother's body. Soon its body parts start to form, and it begins to look more like a cat.

Special delivery
The kitten gets food from its mother's body along a ropelike part known as the cord.

Taking shape
The kitten's head and body grow. Then its eyes, legs, tail, and fur start to form.

HERE I AM!

The time is near for the mother cat to give birth. She is very heavy with the kittens inside her and needs to sleep and rest a lot.

Safe den

The mother cat looks for a quiet, dark place. She needs a safe den where she can give birth to her kittens. It might be a warm closet or an old cardboard box.

One by one

The kittens come out one by one. Giving birth to them all takes the mother cat between one and ten hours.

Clean up

The group, or litter, of kittens are brothers and sisters. The mother cat licks them clean and keeps them warm.

WHAT CAN I DO?

The newborn kitten spends most of its time sleeping and eating. It stays close to its mother and snuggles up with its brothers and sisters to keep warm.

Feeding time

The kitten feeds on milk. It sucks the milk from a nipple on its mother's belly. Each kitten in a litter has its own nipple. It pushes with its front paws to help the milk flow.

Weak and helpless

When the kitten is born, its eyes are closed, it cannot hear, and it isn't strong enough to walk. Its mother moves it by gently picking it up with her mouth.

Newborn noises

Even a newborn kitten can make a noise. It squeaks to tell its mother when it is hungry.

Curious kitten

After about a week, the kitten's eyes start to open. It begins to stretch its legs and to crawl around.

Even an adult cat sleeps for around 18 hours a day—how lazy!

DiscoveryFact™

Squeak!

The kitten's eyes are open.

Growing Fast

By three weeks old, the kitten is starting to walk and run. It's a little wobbly and gets tired quickly—often falling over or flopping down.

Look and listen

By four weeks the kitten can hear and see fairly well. It can see in the dark much better than we can. It also uses its long whiskers to feel its way around in the dark.

The kitten now has sharp teeth.

Weaning

The kitten begins to explore away from its mother. Its teeth are growing. It starts to eat other foods and drinks less of its mother's milk. This time is known as weaning.

PLAYFUL PAWS

Cats are natural hunters—they love to chase and pounce. Kittens learn how to do this by playing.

Exercise is fun!

The kitten loves to explore and play with toys—and anything else it can get its paws on. It needs lots of exercise to make its muscles strong and improve its balance.

A kitten pats a toy.

DiscoveryFact™

Watching mom

The kittens learn from their mother. She plays with them and teaches them everything they need to know. They learn how to keep clean and where to go to the bathroom.

Boo!

Play fight!

The kittens creep up and pounce on anything that moves—often their brothers and sisters!

15

CAT CHAT

Most cats like some company. They love to be with people. If a kitten grows up with other animals—even dogs—they will probably be good friends.

"You're my friend!"
If a cat feels friendly, it rubs itself against its friends and "talks" by meowing.

Let's be friends!

Happy cat
A very happy cat purrs. It might even roll onto its back to have its tummy tickled.

Most wild cats live alone. Lions are the only ones that live and hunt in groups—called prides.

DiscoveryFact™

Hiss!

Stay away

A scared or angry cat flattens its ears and hisses. It may also arch its back, fluff up its fur, and swish its tail.

Look out!

A cat who does not want to be touched may scratch or bite. So be careful!

Time For A Change

When the kitten is 9 to 12 weeks old it will be ready to leave its mother, brothers, and sisters. It's time for the kitten to meet its new family.

Settling in

The new owners must keep the kitten indoors for a few days. The kitten will need some time to settle in and learn where its food, water, and litter box are.

Busy, busy

The kitten needs a lot of attention and plenty of toys to play with.

A kitten uses its teeth to play.

Out and about

Soon the kitten will be ready to go outside. It will love to play and explore, and it won't pay much attention to fences—jumping over them is good exercise!

ON MY OWN

When it is six months old, the cat is almost full-grown. It spends a lot of time outside hunting mice and birds, then comes inside to rest where it's warm.

Feeding time
An adult cat needs one or two meals a day of meat, fish, or canned or dried cat food.

Hunting fun
A well-fed cat hunts for fun, not because it is hungry!

Keeping clean
The cat cleans itself by licking its fur with its rough tongue. If it swallows too much fur it might cough up a slimy lump called a hair ball!

A cat's tongue is covered with little spikes called barbs, which help comb its fur. A lion's tongue is even rougher!

DiscoveryFact™

I'm busy!

ALL GROWN UP

By the time the cat is about one year old, she is an adult cat. She can now have kittens of her own.

Home sweet home

Most adult cats stay in the area around their home—this is their territory. Some toms wander much farther in search of queens to mate with.

Catnaps

A cat has favorite sleeping spots. The older it gets, the more it naps. It may nap for more than half the day.

LIFE CYCLE

Mating
The male and female mate. The kitten starts to grow inside its mother.

Birth
The kitten is born after nine weeks.

1 year
The kitten is now an adult cat. It can have kittens of its own.

First feelings
The kitten purrs, hisses, and squeaks to show its feelings.

6–8 months
The kitten is now almost full-grown.

1–2 weeks
The eyes and ears start to work, and the kitten starts to move around.

9–12 weeks
The kitten can now leave its mother and go to a new home.

2–3 weeks
The kitten's baby teeth start to grow.

9–12 weeks
Play becomes more serious; there may be fights with other cats.

3–4 weeks
The kitten walks and runs. It can use a litter box and clean itself.

8–9 weeks
All the kitten's baby teeth have grown. Its eyes are their adult color.

From 5 weeks
The kitten stops feeding on its mother's milk and eats solid food.